Enlightenment Made Easy

Discovering The Obvious

Dr. David Parrish

www.davidparrish.us

ACKNOWLEDGEMENTS

I am deeply grateful to have had the benefit of many teachers, teachings, and practices over the years. I am particularly grateful to Werner Erhard for creating a language to access the field of human experience. I am also grateful to have come upon Douglas Harding's experiments and his vision of enlightenment.

This project was inspired by the conversations with Richard Lang and friends from around the world in online meetings to reflect and share about the experience of conscious awareness that Douglas Harding called "The Headless Way."

Many thanks to Ange Chianese, Travis Eneix, April Leffler, and Nancy

Margalit for the work they contributed to the content and editing of this book.

Finally I give deep thanks to my wife Dr. Christie Parrish for her consistent expression of love, and specifically for tolerating my states of mind as I passed through my personal bardo over the last year.

FORWARD

My experience of Who I am includes many voices – I am part of a world-wide community of friends who are awake to Who they really are, and who, when they can, enjoy hanging out with one another and exchanging views about their True Nature – about our True Nature. We are many voices in one Consciousness.

David Parrish is one of these friends, one of these voices. In this book he shares his own unique response to discovering the One we all really are. He speaks with passion. He wants to share the Treasure he has found because he knows first-hand that it is true, and that it is valuable – valuable in a practical everyday way. Valuable in terms of having better relationships, valuable in terms of coping with loss, in terms of facing problems and ultimately in terms of facing death. And as he says, it doesn't matter what you call it – enlightenment is just a word. The thing is to have the experience. And so, David invites you to look at the place you are looking out of. Not to think about what you really are at your own centre, but simply to look, and to trust what you find – or what you don't find.

I hope you will look, with David and myself and countless others – look at the One who is looking. As David indicates, when you turn your attention round 180 degrees, you don't see your face. You don't see anything. But here's the wonder and delight – what fills this Nothingness is Everything. Don't miss out on being this Awake Nothing that is Everything!

I wish David success with making more Seeing friends through this book.

Richard Lang

INTRODUCTION

I have been a psychologist for over twenty-five years. During this time, I worked full time in a state prison system. The prison work provided me with the opportunity to learn about confinement.

Confinement involves living in a highly controlled environment, feeling threatened most of the time, waiting for a better future, and using whatever is available to distract oneself from the present situation.

Early on, I realized that although I walked out of the prison everyday, I was living in confinement. I realized that the prison most of us inhabit is one we carry around with us and that we delude ourselves into thinking we are free while we pretend that we are ok. This prison is a state of mind.

A human being is a part of the whole that we call the universe, a part limited in time and space. He experiences himself, his thoughts and feelings, as something separated from the rest — a kind of optical illusion of his consciousness. This illusion is a prison for us, restricting us to our personal desires and to affection for only the few people nearest us. Our task must be to free ourselves from this prison ...

Albert Einstein

The prison occurs as a voice in our head that we relate to as "me thinking." This voice is constantly chattering, and most of what it is saying is neurotic ruminating generated as a commentary on whatever is happening. We can't get away from this voice; it comes with us where ever we go. We confuse thinking with reality and consistently react to life in ways that are detrimental to ourselves and others. I saw that my ways of being and acting in the world were determined by this self-righteous, judgmental, fearful "me" that somehow I was being subjected to. In my head there was the me that was doing the talking (the voice in my head), and the me who was listening—the prisoner of the voice in my head. As crazy as this sounds, I was aware that I was no more insane than everyone else, because I had always heard others make comments like, "I thought to myself" or "What was I thinking?" Somehow we consistently ignore that this is an indication that there is something happening that has very negative implications. The "me" doing the talking was making the "me" doing the listening miserable. With this recognition, I set out looking for liberation. I had heard of enlightenment and that it was about freedom from the suffering of the confinement of a typical human life—the confinement of living in a reactive state of mind, compulsively judging everything and trying to control and improve life. A good example of this is something as simple as the weather. The weather occurs for most of us as a judgment: good weather or bad weather. If it's raining that's bad, and if it is sunny that's good. The same with time: we are having a good time or a bad time rather than just experiencing the arising and passing of experiences. It occurred to me that if enlightenment could offer a way of being relaxed, enjoying life, and enjoying myself, it was worth looking into.

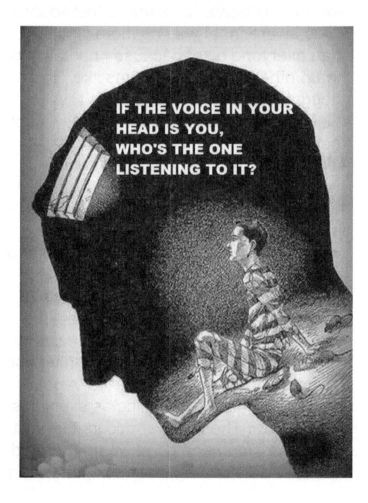

IF THE VOICE IN YOUR HEAD IS YOU, WHO'S THE ONE LISTENING TO IT?

Many of the traditions that speak of enlightenment teach that it is an attainment that requires great sacrifice, a monastic lifestyle, and many years of work to cleanse the mind. However, in other traditions such as Zen, enlightenment is spoken of as a sudden awakening to a direct experience of being conscious and aware. This is the enlightenment that is presented here. It is an immediate personal and direct experience that gives us a completely new perspective.

After decades of doing everything I could to move forward on a path to what seemed to be enlightenment, I was not optimistic about being enlightened in this lifetime. I wasn't even sure what enlightenment actually was other than what I had heard and read about.

Then one day, I don't recall exactly when, I saw it, and it was clear to me that enlightenment is always available to us all. I saw that time had nothing to do with it. I also saw that the root cause of human suffering is delusion, ignorance of the truth of what we are and the truth of reality. When I say truth, I simply mean the experience of reality versus the commonly held concepts and beliefs about what is real. The reality that is a direct experience. A concept is a thought about experience, and if we don't notice that a thought is an interpretation, we are ignoring the experience and considering the thought to be the reality. You can't eat the thought "hamburger," in the same way you can't experience what you are as a thought. Having seen beyond the concept of myself and having experienced this awake, alive, and immediately real be-ing, I knew that there was nothing more important for me to do than to practice living this and share this in my work with people.

To be clear, I have used the word enlightenment for its value in capturing something that human beings want. Although the word enlightenment is often associated with Eastern philosophies and mystical notions, it also seems to refer to an experience that is beyond the common human condition of discontent, worry, concern, hope, and fear. This experience could be described as a kind of freedom in which there is contentment, a being at ease, a feeling of being at home in one's body, an experience of joy, and love of life.

I see all of humanity seeking this experience in many different forms. Some of the ways that this condition of suffering is commonly thought to be relieved are through the accumulation of money and material wealth, power and control, and belief in religious, political, or philosophical ideas.

I am not intending to claim that the enlightenment I am talking about in this book is the instantaneous and permanent transformation that the word is often taken to mean. The enlightenment I claim to be easy is the simple and direct perception which is conscious awareness itself. I assert that this perception is easy because it is noticing a view that has been here since birth for all of us that has been overlaid by our conditioned or learned perceptions. And although I am not talking about a complete and total transformation, I do assert that this direct way of seeing is the beginning of such a transformation. In a sense, this transformation begins with directly seeing that we are not the entity given a name and an orientation in a body, which is the common beginning of "knowing who we are." The form of the "self" when seen directly "transitions" from a "self concept" to an experience of "immediate being," and thus a "transformation" begins to occur.

While this direct "seeing" is a discovery, what is discovered has been present since our incarnation (consciousness arising in the flesh), and is present in all other beings. This is the reason I say enlightenment is easy. It is easy because all that is needed is to give attention to the experience of conscious awareness itself as it presently exists. It is already the case that we are free, and it was never the case that we were other than this open and free, conscious, aware be-ing.

I have written this book to assert that enlightenment is available to any and all human beings, and to provide the opportunity for the reader to enjoy and share the experience of "seeing," which is the perception of the actual view of self and the world. This seeing is enlightenment. Prior to seeing, the world occurs as "reality": the only reality. After seeing, the world occurs as an ever-changing projected virtual appearance.

It is my intention to present a variety of ideas about enlightenment that have the potential of having the reader distinguish, notice, and be familiar with this perception. Language is complicated and is a crude method for the transmission of experience, yet it is what we have to work with, and so the words will serve as pointers to what is beyond words. This I think is why Jesus spoke in parables and why poetry is more useful than common talk to point to an experience as abstract as enlightenment. Enlightenment is easy to "get" since it is already the case, but it is not so easy to describe or explain. If it were easy to describe and explain, everybody would just learn about it and readily see it. It is something like quantum science. The idea that there is no actual material world, and that the world occurs as a function of looking at it is difficult to get.[1] Even Einstein had difficulty digesting it. It is also like time: the idea that everything is happening now and that now is the only reality there is, is so counterintuitive that we simply don't pay much attention to it (at our great expense).

In the case of enlightenment, you must be your own authority in the matter of seeing it. This is not a case of "seeing is believing." This is a matter of "believing what you're seeing." Actually, enlightenment is unbelievable in that to believe what is directly seen is like adding more of the color red to the color red. As one teacher stated, "The truth believed is a lie."

The experience of experiencing consciousness as it is, unconditioned, and free of any form or content, is completely subjective. It cannot be taught or learned as an objective reality because consciousness does not occur in the world; rather, the world occurs in consciousness. Human consciousness is a singular first person experience, and while we can share it, we are alone as it is. Said another way, it alone exists; it is one.

The opportunity that enlightenment offers is to be free from the prison of the mind, to be aware of the mind and no longer identified with it. This opens up a new realm of possibilities. Reactive thoughts and feelings will still occur, but they no longer automatically determine behavior. This is a radical shift that can make a profound difference in everyday life. This is the hallmark of a mature human being.

This book is for people who may have heard of enlightenment and are curious about it, or perhaps interested in considering the possibility of being enlightened. It may also be of use for people who have been involved in seeking enlightenment but feel that they have not experienced it. Finally, this book may be of value to people who have experienced enlightenment, as a means to further enjoy the nature of the experience, make use of ways to think about, talk about or share it, and experience the process that lies ahead.

Enlightenment is a loaded word that has taken on so many meanings that most people who talk about this experience now typically use other words that point to the same thing: words such as "awakening" and "self-realization." However, the words don't really matter. It is the experience that counts. I really don't care about the word pizza. What I care about is the experience of eating it. If you have the experience referred to here as enlightenment, you will care as little as I do about what it is called.

What we all want is an enlightened life, and an enlightened world, and it starts with being an enlightened being, which is actually a matter of looking, seeing, and choosing.

Living an enlightened life is the actual prize—the fulfillment of the possibility of a human life....*to be aware of awareness itself as life.* It is the actualization of being human, and yet it is ordinary and easily mistaken because it is not a matter of content or appearance. It is a matter of context. Context is the key, in that rather than anything changing, the context in which things occur has what is being perceived "appear" differently, so that we relate differently to what we see. When you recognize the old woman you had hateful thoughts about because she was driving so slow in front of you in traffic is your grandmother, the context changes in an instant.

Context makes all the difference. It is like watching a movie, in that we are free to allow ourselves to experience fear, sadness, anger, and all sorts of drama because it is in the context of a harmless image on the screen. Enlightenment is the context of all contexts. As such, it is a way of seeing that is free from fear and open to all of life as it is. It is the mother of all experiences, and until enlightenment is experienced, life occurs as happening to us. After enlightenment, life occurs as moving through us.

The greatest obstacle to experiencing enlightenment is its obviousness. The second obstacle is the notion that enlightenment has any particular form, feels any particular way, or changes anything. At the same time, enlightenment changes everything. It is a context for living that provides a clear way of being and way of seeing reality as it is, so that living skillfully occurs as a natural process.

This book is not written with the intent to take the reader through a process or reach a conclusion. It is not meant to go anywhere. It is meant to present the opportunity to notice where you already are. You are already conscious, and you are already experiencing the eternal now. One sure way to miss this is to attempt to get somewhere other than here and now. After presenting a simple experiment to point to the experience, I will present and respond to questions that are typically asked to assist in distinguishing the nature of "seeing." It is suggested that the reader start with the first chapter and do the experiment, which is a very simple way to have the direct experience of what is being distinguished here as enlightenment.

In keeping with the intent of this book, the easiest way to get enlightenment is simply to experience it. That may sound a bit weird because most people would say, "That is obvious, but how do I do that?" This book will provide the opportunity.

While this experience is always available, most of us are oriented to *not noticing* it due to our common way of being as an identity. That is, we identify with being a body, a unique self or personality, with a unique experience of the world. Nonetheless, it is a simple matter to see that you are enlightened.

I invite you to engage in this opportunity to see what you are and to entertain the possibility of living an enlightened life. It is my vision that we all dare to be enlightened, and to love life as a magical and mysterious ride.

---

[1] https://en.wikipedia.org/wiki/Double-slit_experiment

Getting It

A Few Prerequisites To Consider

While experiencing enlightenment is easy, the pointers and examples presented to give access to the experience are much more useful when conditioned ways of perceiving, attending, and being are noticed and relaxed. Our typical "fixed" ways of encountering experiences are reactive and dependent on the perception fitting our previous conditioning. However, it is possible to notice this and thereby be aware of what is being missed. Usually, when we encounter a perception, we have a recognition; that is, we re-cognize what is there. Recognition is a thought occurring that identifies what is there based on past learning. To see what will be pointed to as enlightenment we must be willing to notice that *there is no recognition of that which is being looked at. It is the only perception that you can have that cannot be referenced with any past learning or previous perception. In a sense it is the perception of perception.*

Seeing enlightenment is totally dependent on "present evidence." So the following prerequisites are preparation for this unique experience.

Getting It as a Way of Listening

In order to open you up to seeing how easy being enlightened actually is, it is necessary to re-define listening in a unique way. You may have come across the saying, "Let those who have ears hear." Obviously, this is not referring to physical ears. Rather, it is referring to what I call "listening." Usually what people consider listening is simply hearing what is said or reading what is written, as in this case. However, what actually occurs is that we hear our interpretation of what is said or what we read. There is a process that is always going on in our heads, so we might not notice it. It is the processing of what we hear in terms of whether it fits what we already know. We call this "understanding." Another part of this process is judgment and evaluation; we decide whether we agree with what is said or with what we are reading. This all happens in a matter of seconds, and most of us are not aware that this is different from "getting what was stated." At best, what we get is some version of what was presented with a judgment and evaluation attached. The problem with this is that we typically don't notice the process, so we simply think we are hearing what was communicated.

If I am to be successful in communicating with you in a way that will be useful in providing access to the experience of enlightenment, I must request that the way you listen to what you're reading is to simply "get it," versus being concerned about whether you understand it, like it, or agree with it.

Since the way we typically do what we call listening is automatic, and since we have been listening this way for so long, it isn't realistic to attempt to just stop and switch to listening by just "getting" exactly what is communicated. However, what you can do is to notice the processing and see the difference between what was communicated and what you had it mean or whether you agree with it.

This business of "getting it" is simple and yet very powerful; however, it requires that you pay attention to exactly what is communicated . For example, if I say, "The sky is blue," "getting it" would be that you notice anything that gets added or subtracted from the statement. So if what you get is "The sky is blue, and so what?" or "The sky is blue and I don't like blue," then you did not "get it."

This may seem to be a sidetrack, but I promise you it is critical to experiencing being enlightened. The reason that this is so is that in order for you to experience being enlightened you must look for it in your own experience. I can guide you to do this by giving you hints and ideas of what to look for. However, if you don't get exactly what I am distinguishing, then you will be looking for something other than what I am pointing toward. In a sense, in order to experience being enlightened, you must get out of the way. Now that was just something to get. Please notice whether you added, "What does he mean by that?" or "What does that mean?" Or you might think, "How do I get out of my own way?" It is totally OK if you had any of those thoughts. Just notice that and "get," "*In a sense, in order to experience being enlightened, you must get out of the way.*"

So, now you might ask, "If I just 'get' what is communicated, what do I do with it?" The answer is: in order to notice what is being pointed at, just be related to it, just be with it, just have it and be present to it. Its like a joke, when you just "get" the punchline you see something that you did not expect. Experiencing enlightenment is much like this.

I will be presenting a number of different ways of hinting and pointing to "It," (the experience of enlightenment) as you just keep "getting" what is said and looking at your experience. At some point "It" will become evident, not because it is hidden, but rather because you had not yet noticed it. I will say more about this later. So, for you to experience enlightenment, you must follow the instructions. That is, you must "get" exactly what is said and then look at your experience to see what is pointed out or distinguished. This is a fail-proof way of experiencing enlightenment. I will share how that is the case later on in the book.

For now just be clear about "getting it," "got it?"

Can I Have Your Attention Please?

The next important aspect of experiencing enlightenment is to direct your attention to specific areas in the field of your experience. I will give you specific ideas of what to notice or look at and consider, and unless you consciously and intentionally direct your attention to what is distinguished as it occurs in the field of your experience, you will miss it.

The default state for human beings is ignorance. This is not a put down; it is simply what is so, and to see the fact of this and accept it is very powerful. Ignorance is simply a matter of ignoring most of what occurs in the field of experience. Our brain does this to filter out the incoming information that is not relevant to the task at hand and to our survival. It is often the case that people consider ignorance to be a fault. In this process of seeing, ignorance is a simple matter of not noticing, and is almost always due to being distracted or preoccupied, or simply unaware.

The practice of directing attention and using attention in a specific way is essential not only to experiencing being enlightened, but in practicing living in an enlightened way, which is the curriculum for those who have experienced enlightenment.

Without experiencing that you are enlightened, there is no possibility for living in an enlightened way, because the world of being enlightened does not appear to exist. Prior to enlightenment, there is one world. After enlightenment, there are two worlds: the one you're in, and the one in you. Then, If you pay attention and do your homework, it becomes clear that the two worlds are one and that you are both in the world and the world is in you. This may not make any sense to you at the moment, but as you proceed this will become evident. And it is one of those "just get it" communications. So, "just get it" and move on.

The way to practice directing attention begins with noticing that you're not directing attention. Just as in the case with listening, to notice that listening is consistently distorted makes it possible to listen accurately. Noticing that your attention is constantly distracted provides the opportunity to direct and focus attention. Anyone who has attempted to simply hold attention on the breath for any period of time has discovered how little control most people have with attention.

Being attentive is another aspect of living an enlightened life. However, to "see" from an enlightened view, it is sufficient that you simply follow the suggestion to pay attention to what is distinguished as it occurs in your experience.

Being Open

The third prerequisite and the most important one is the state of "being open." This state is a state of being receptive and accepting to what occurs or appears in the field of experience. This state is a state of heart and a state of mind. The experience of enlightenment is an experience of being open. When the experience of being enlightened is present, this state of being open is natural and simply the way it is. However, if we limit ourselves to only accepting what fits our existing version of reality, our beliefs, and concepts about the way things are, we will not notice what is directly in front of our eyes. People who have experienced enlightenment are called seers because they have noticed what is always there but missed or ignored by most of humanity. As is the case with listening and with attention, being open involves noticing the various ways in which we are constrained, contracted, or withheld. This requires a willingness to "let go." "Letting go" is letting go of thinking as a way of being and experiencing what cannot be put into words. You are not who you think you are. In fact you cannot "think" who you are. Enlightenment is non-verbal, non-conceptual, unconditioned, direct, and personal. Enlightenment is secular. It is not religious, philosophical, or mysterious. It is simple and obvious, and it is the natural state of being human.

Being open is an act of will. This openness to what appears in the field of consciousness has been called "Beginner's Mind." One is open out of the simple willingness to be open. This state of being is very useful in order to have the experience of enlightenment, and after experiencing enlightenment, it becomes another part of the curriculum of the human experience and a key aspect of living an enlightened life.

Doing Nothing

The experience of enlightenment is not a function of doing anything. You cannot do anything to be what you already are. It is a matter of directing attention to the actual phenomenon of being conscious. Consciousness is what it is like to be you. This is not typically the way we experience who we are. We typically operate with an ongoing self-concept that we are so used to as an identity that most of us never question who we are. There is a mental process that is constantly producing the perception of everything that comes into our awareness as that which is happening to us. It is apparent when we speak and use the word "I" and "my" and "mine" that we are always operating as an identity that is generated in thought. "I" think is what we say when thoughts occur. We automatically consider thoughts to be coming from us, even though we don't know what we think until we look at the thought that occurred: *a thought that we did not know until it appeared in the mind.* The identity is conditioned to perceive that in order to have an outcome, in this case be enlightened, it requires doing something, taking some kind of action. When the question is asked, "How **do** I experience enlightenment?" the question is asking about what to do. When doing nothing is seen from an enlightened view, it is clear that *nothing is what is doing*, even in the midst of intense activity. (Just get that.) This will be evident upon noticing enlightenment.

Getting Nowhere Fast

A guide to direct experience

Now that we have set up some prerequisites that relax the filtering of experience, we can get to the looking to notice the experience of being enlightened.

The purpose of what is written here is to stimulate you to notice what is the most obvious and evident experience you will ever have.

I have made it a point to limit references to existing traditions and practices associated with enlightenment in this book so as to avoid associating this simple yet profound experience with so many of the typical "spiritual" notions that have turned enlightenment into a "special" mystical state. There is nothing that anyone can tell you that will result in your experiencing enlightenment. The experience of enlightenment is a state of being that is revealed by seeing. This seeing is a matter of noticing what is always there and accepting it as it is. When you experience enlightenment, it will be an experience you notice at will. Enlightenment is a discovery.

One specific reference I will make in this book is to a number of experiments that a man who was a philosopher and a pioneer in the technology of human consciousness invented. His experiments provide the opportunity to have a direct experience of enlightenment. He didn't often call the experience enlightenment, most likely to avoid the problems associated with such a loaded term. His name was Douglas Harding, and he simply wanted to have a direct experience of what he was. He called the experience he stumbled upon "Having No Head." He noticed that he could not see his head directly and came upon a view from where he was looking that revealed a completely unique experience. It was clear to him that this experience was the same as all of the accounts he had heard of what being enlightened was like. Douglas created a number of experiments that provided direct access to this experience and spent the remainder of his life sharing what he had discovered.

I won't go into details about Douglas Harding; the reader can easily find his work online.[1] I will use an experiment that he invented that I consider to be the most simple and direct method to provide an opportunity to "notice" what Harding noticed. Then, I will continue to point to what can be said about this experience so as to address confusion or interpretations of the experience that may hinder the recognition of what is called enlightenment.

The key to this experiment is to actually do it and simply *take what you get*. This is a non-verbal, and personal, experience.

---

[1]. www.headless.org

The Pointing Experiment

This is the basic experiment that Douglas Harding created. It is very simple and easy to do, and you cannot do it wrong. Remember, the key to "getting" the experience the experiment brings to your attention to notice is to simply follow directions and take what you get.

1. Point to an object in your immediate location.
2. Notice that what you're pointing at is a thing, some-thing, you may say or think what it is.
3. Now point at your foot. Notice that this is a thing. A part of your body.
4. Now point at your chest area. Notice that this is a thing, another part of your body.
5. Now move your finger up toward your face and notice that at a point above your chest that you can no longer see any "*thing*."
6. Now move your finger directly in front of your eyes.
7. *What is you finger pointing at?*

You have just experienced enlightenment, and you have either "got that" or you had a thought about it, or your attention shifted to your finger.

If you did not "get it," it is because you did not accept it as it is. If you looked at what your finger was pointing to when you pointed it to what is looking, and you accepted it as it is, then you would SEE it. If you had a thought that you did not see anything because, unless you see SOMETHING it does not exist , then you were ignoring your own experience. This does not make you bad or wrong. Most people in the world don't accept that "nothing" exists, even though this *leaves them without a home.* (Just get that.)

Now here is the deal. You just pointed at who or what you are, (no-thing, space, emptiness) and who or what you are is enlightened (free and complete). So when you notice it, you are experiencing being enlightened. Can it be that simple? Yes, it is that simple. Enlightenment is the experience of being you, and you are already you and you are already enlightened (free). As one great teacher said, "*What you are looking for is what is looking.*" Said another way you are consciousness…that which never moves or is ever touched by what occurs in it.

To quote Douglas Harding on this:

"It's a cosmic happening and bears no date. No human, as such, was ever enlightened, for enlightenment is seeing that you aren't so much a human being as plain being. And no being, as such, was ever *un*enlightened, for Being is enlightenment. It follows that the enlightenment of one is the enlightenment of all (past, present, or future) and just can't be contained."

Of course, all of the concepts, distinctions, and descriptions above are secondary to the experience, and what is really cool and begins to open the possibility of living a new life is the view from this experience.

The view from this experience is reality. You don't have to believe it; you're seeing it. From this view when you turn your head, the world moves. We share the habit of considering our body to be moving; however, based on the evidence, it is clear that *we never move*. Just play around with this a bit and notice it. When you are walking, notice the ground moving under you. When you are driving in a car, notice the scenery moving past you. This is what I referred to earlier as life moving through you, rather than happening to you. From this view, or more accurately from this perception, since it is not just visual, everything changes but you. This experience of being is mysterious...it just is. It is all inclusive (everything in the universe appears here) and yet it is no thing.

You may feel some confusion, because human beings are generally in a state of confusion. We confuse who and what we are with that which appears to be us. Human beings are given an identity early on in life, and this identity is so complete and so consistent with the way that all other human beings are being that it immediately becomes who we think we are. We notice that there is a body that we appear to inhabit (I will provide the opportunity to notice otherwise), we are given a name, and we consider our signature to symbolize us. When we show ID, it has a picture of our head (the only perception of our head we ever have is indirect). We begin to get names for every other person and thing in the world. Once we get enough language and orientation to function, we start school, where we learn what we need to know to continue on in life and behave "normally." That is... to be like everybody else who does not know who they really are and continue to ignore it. You see, this is the trick I made reference to earlier. If almost everyone thinks they know who they are, based on the information they were given, and thinks the world is the way it appears, based on the information given, then it appears "real" and occurs as all there is. Reality is a matter of agreement. If enough people agree on something, it is considered "knowledge." Even if it involves burning people at the stake because they are witches. Just like the magic tricks, our attention is taken by the appearance of what is happening rather than by what is actually there. Enlightenment is seeing clearly that an appearance is an appearance. And, when we see how obvious the way most magic tricks or illusions work, it is clear how easy it is to mis-take who we are, especially given that we learn who we are as children from people we are dependent on and trust.

You may recall that a reference was made to enlightenment as an experience of freedom or liberation. Enlightenment is the experience that you are not *a thing*. The experience that you are not a thing is an experience of *being no thing*, or simply the experience of nothing. This experience liberates you from "thingness." A body is a thing, it grows up, it grows old, it dies. Consciousness is no-thing, it does not change, it does not age, it does not die, it is not in time; therefore, it did not start—it just happens. So the you that you have considered yourself to be was never you and does not actually exist; *therefore, you were never born and can never die.* I know that is not the habitual way it occurs for you. However, with the repeated noticing of the "it," "it" will become familiar and provide you with the opportunity to see this way consistently. Living an enlightened life is the practice of being who you really are.

Let me distinguish this natural state of being further so that you can take note of its presence and its nature.

That which you pointed at is always there, whether you look to notice it or not.

Upon direct experience it is clear that it does not move, it has no desire, no form, and no direction. It is open to whatever appears in its view. It only exists in the present, and it has no thoughts or feelings. You do not have it... **you are it**. Said more directly, "It just is." It is non-dual. This reveals the problem of the voice in your head. That voice is not you: it is thought, and it occurs as a necessary process to function in the world. Neurosis - a relatively mild mental illness that is not caused by organic disease - involving symptoms of stress (depression, anxiety, obsessive behavior, hypochondria) is a result of identifying with thought. Once this is seen, thoughts lose the power to disrupt and disturb and are seen as either useful or not useful.

Another way to distinguish this experience is to notice that anything that can be seen, thought of, or spoken of is not it. When we attempt to look at it, we notice that *we don't see it because it is us looking*. Therefore it occurs to us as nothing.

The Identity, the me, or "self" exists only as a concept, idea, thought, memory, or projection into the future. The self occurs to us primarily in the form of a body. When we imagine ourselves in memories or in fantasies of the future, we perceive ourselves as a body with a head and a face, and yet we never actually see our own head or face other than as a reflection. This is what Douglas Harding referred to as being headless. You will never directly see your head. You cannot see what is looking; therefore, you cannot be anything you can look at.

One way of distinguishing this "being" is to notice that it has never aged. It feels the same as it did when we were five years old. This is an interesting aspect of the experience of aging. We notice our bodies changing, but that which is noticing is not changing. The reactions about the appearance of the body only occur out of the identification with it, and thus our identification with its eventual demise.

If this all occurs as strange, weird, or difficult that is because we are trying to get at something that is not some-thing. In fact it is the only point of existence that is not a thing. If we symbolized it with a digit it would be zero.

Be-ing is a verb

The experience of being is always happening. It started when we were born. We were just being natural as infants being infants, without language, full of life, interacting with whatever occurred. Then we began to learn about who we were, and this is when we took on an identity and we lost the state of being that was happening and did not notice losing it. The way it occurred for us was that we accepted what the people who were here before us said about who we are, and about the world we are living in. This quickly became our default way of being and seemed so real that we never questioned it. It occurred for us that it was just the way it is, and there was nothing other than that. Many of us live out our entire lives in this state of mind, and we deal with life and its challenges by believing in more of what we learn from those who came before, and from the specific ways of processing the ongoing information available all around us. Of course, this is necessary and appropriate in order to function in the world. However, it leaves us without a ground of being, and it sentences us to repeating the same mistakes of previous generations. It leaves us limited to only what can be learned from outside of ourselves. It leaves us limited to what can be known in language or symbols rather than by direct experience. This becomes so completely the way it all occurs that for the most part we don't know the difference between concepts and experience. We don't know the difference between our "self-concept" and the moment to moment experience of "being." Enlightenment could be defined as *the experience of being.* It's the same experience of being that you had as a child, except that now *it is possible to notice it because you have been being some "thing" other than it*, which makes *it* distinct and noticeable. An infant has no other way of being until it is named and joins the world of "things." This way of being a some "thing," a some "body," this personhood and way of life that goes with it, totally occupy our attention so that the unconditioned experience of being that is always happening goes unnoticed. It is something like breathing. Breathing is constant, it is always happening and is easy to not notice. Even things that are very consistent in our experience, such as driving a car, become so automatic that we can have conversations or be occupied by thoughts about other things while doing it. The experience of being *is the most constant aspect of the human experience* —more constant than breathing. When we look, we notice breathing because the breath moves in and out. "Being" *never moves so it is easy not only not to notice it, but to notice it and not see it.* This is another reason that people who experience enlightenment are called seers. They see who/what they are and this perception gives them access to an experience much larger that the named person with a conditioned mind and brain operating in life as a personality. Most people think they have a personality and don't realize they are "being" a personality. Once "seeing" occurs, it becomes possible to notice that a personality is a collection of data held together by the notion that the data describes who you are and verifies that you exist. Seeing involves being clear that the you that appeared to be who you are is a convention for operating in the world. A name with a body associated with it is a set of patterns of behavior and a story that distinguishes one person from another. The value of experiencing enlightenment is the discovery that you are not who you think you are and that *what you are is experience itself.* Said another way, you are the space or clearing in which the universe is occurring, including the sun, the moon, all of humanity, and the "little you personality" being used to play out dramas and scripts. I say "little personality" because upon experiencing the truth of self, the personality occurs as a little you that isn't taken so seriously any longer. In fact, the data that is required to run a personality by the brain has been estimated by neuroscientists to be small enough to be held on a thumb drive. Upon experiencing enlightenment, it is evident that, rather than you moving through life, or space, or time, it is life, space, and time that are moving through you.

Many have experienced enlightenment accidentally, in the sense that they were not trying to experience it. Often in situations where a person is in extreme despair, they notice that which is never affected by circumstances….the direct experience of being. It occurs in the blink of an eye, and it may last for various periods; however, for most it passes, and we find ourselves back in our ordinary way of being. Many read books, follow teachers, teachings, and practices for many years and do not notice the experience of enlightenment. You cannot learn enlightenment and there is no practice that will increase your potential to experience enlightenment. One reason for this is that, if enlightenment is considered something that is not happening now, then it is sought in the future, when actually it is always only happening now. Another reason for this seeking and not finding is that enlightenment is the most ordinary experience a human being can have, and if it is considered a special state, or a special experience involving constant bliss, or visions, or special powers, it will be missed. There are many who isolate or live a monastic life, and while this may be useful for training the mind or for experiencing very subtle forms of energy, it does not necessarily produce an experience of enlightenment and may become a major barrier to the experience. *Every human being is equally capable at all times of experiencing enlightenment.*

Enlightenment is the Experience of Nothing. (No-thing)

This is not the definition you will find in any dictionary I have come across. However, if this book is to succeed in its promise to make enlightenment easy, it will be necessary to get right to the essence of the matter. It will give us a target to shoot for, and set up having the experience of nothing be easy.

You may already be reacting to this definition. It seems the human mind has little tolerance for "nothing." However I assure you "nothing" matters. In fact, as you will see if you take the trip, nothing is actually the source of everything.

If we are going to make enlightenment easy, then we are going to have to deal with the common insistence on making sense and being rational and reasonable. The easy way to enlightenment is the direct way. It is the direct experience that comes prior to thinking, and it doesn't fit any system of thought like rational thought, logical thought, or reasoning of any kind.

Essentially, enlightenment is about freedom and transformation. It is an experience of being free from a condition in which happiness and well-being appear to be elusive. Enlightenment is actually the experience that all human beings desire. It is an experience of being alive, satisfied, content, and fulfilled that is available to all human beings; and yet only a very few have this experience. Enlightenment is power. Being enlightened is being free to see life clearly and to act skillfully as we endeavor to participate in the human experience. Another useful way to define what I am calling enlightenment is to look into your own experience and notice if there is a sense of longing for being totally at home in your skin and in your life. That longing and all of the behaviors that it drives are a felt sense of the possibility for realizing the experience of happiness and well-being that are associated with enlightenment.

For most of us, the experience of being happy is elusive and depends on circumstances. Being enlightened allows us to experience happiness at will so that happiness is not dependent on the right circumstances. Being enlightened empowers us to have access to our ways of being and acting so that we are not stuck with our reactive emotions and automatic behaviors. Clearly, enlightenment as it is defined here is a highly desirable experience, which explains why so many people seek it and follow those who claim to have experienced it and offer a path or method to attain it.

While what I will share with you in these pages is not automatically going to give you an experience of enlightenment, what it will do is save you the trouble of spending tons of energy and years of your life seeking it and make enlightenment immediately available to you for the taking.

Discovering the nature of enlightenment is similar to finding out how a magic trick is done. When you see what is actually happening, it appears obvious, and you realize it was really just a matter of your attention being taken by the magician. However, in this case, the trick is being conjured up by billions of us all of the time, and this trick is what has enlightenment seem so illusive. The code name for the trick is "reality." What is generally considered to be reality is a perceptual trick, and the best part of the trick is you. You are the best part of the trick because the core illusion of the appearance of reality is the belief that there is an identity that exists other than the experience of conscious awareness itself. Upon examination, it is evident that while we may operate with the idea that "I" am conscious, when we simply look at what is there in awareness, there is no I, and yet we live as this "I" or "me," and the experience we have of life appears to depend on the condition of this "I." So we don't experience life happening—we experience life happening to "me" and we take everything personally. When a shift occurs in which life is just happening rather than happening to me, life can be taken as it is and we can travel much lighter. Another way of distinguishing enlightenment is that it is the experience of seeing what is so as it is directly, rather than after interpretation.

Another Shot at "It"

If your are still not clear about enlightenment and didn't get it with the pointing experiment, or if you did and you lost it, or if you did and you are trying to keep it, here are some more distinctions that may be of use.

When you "get" enlightenment, you get what you already got.

The cosmic joke is that there is nothing to get. So, you are already enlightened—you cannot be unenlightened. You already are who you are, and you are being who you are. *It is being who you're not that gets in the way.*

Whenever you are totally engaged with an activity and all your attention is on it, you are not self conscious; in other words, your identity is not in awareness, and there is the experience of the lightness of being. Identity is never actually present, it must be generated in thought.

When *you (identity)* are not here…

YOU (present experience) are here.

Being enlightened looks like the way it is for you right now. If you "think" being enlightened is a particular experience that feels a particular way, that is not enlightenment. Enlightenment is the ordinary experience of being which is always still and silent and includes all forms changing constantly.

The only barrier that completely ensures that you won't experience enlightenment is the belief that you are not enlightened.

How Do I Know if I am Enlightened?

Enlightenment is an experience, and in order to know anything it must be put into the form of concepts and language, which comes after the experience. Everything written about enlightenment is not true. The truth of consciousness is an experience and only an experience. So, you cannot know you're enlightened, and yet you can "be" enlightened, and see clearly that you have always been enlightened. To say it more precisely: the you that is enlightened is not the you who wants to know if you're enlightened. The you that is enlightened *doesn't have questions*. This is why, if you really "get" that you are enlightened, there is no further "seeking." Seekers are people who are ignoring the obvious.

Another way to answer this is with another question. "How do you know you're here?" Obviously, you know you're here because it is something that you are experiencing directly. Since there is nothing to it, its existence is self-referential. If there is nothing to get, and you got nothing when you pointed toward consciousness, then you are enlightened.

If you noticed noticing, you saw, seeing, thus awareness is aware of itself as itself.

Another way of dealing with knowing is "knowing from." If you know from identity, that is, you know what you're not, then you are being the seer, because you know the difference between just seeing and seeing and interpreting, which is what the identity always does. The identity confuses interpretations for perceptions. Most people think that what they think is what is so; that is, they think that a thought is a perception. This is dangerous, to say the least. Most people "think" they know who they are even though when challenged about this they cannot give a realistic answer. As an identity the only answers to the question "Who are you?" are identity answers such as a human being, a citizen of the planet, a human body, a mother, father, sister, brother. And then there are the spiritual identities, like "I am a spirit, energetic entity, devotee, expression of the divine, child of God." Many people are preoccupied with seeking as a sophisticated form of denial. They don't really want to find out who they are and deal with fear or the work it takes to live an enlightened life. In a sense, being enlightened involves giving up or surrendering the idea that you're not enlightened. Life will help in this work, because to be stuck in denial and stuck in a personality gets more painful and involves more suffering as time passes.

A few words of caution about enlightenment. Attention is very highly conditioned to be drawn to what is moving, and human beings are oriented to operate "in the world." So it is inevitable that what is noticed when attention is turned 180 degrees will return to the background. This is not at all evidence that you lost enlightenment or that you are not enlightened. Many people come upon enlightenment and think that unless it continues to be the way they perceive consistently that it is not enlightenment. The heart of the matter of enlightenment is that which is the truth of you has no preferences. Human suffering is a result of wanting rather then having. If you want what you have, you have what you want. Given that you will always only have what you have, to say yes to it is the only sane way to live. Equanimity is the essence of open heart and open mind that unfolds from enlightenment. So a realistic way of being certain that you are enlightened is to recognize that you see the human condition as it is and experience a natural interest in expressing the qualities of your authentic nature. Enlightenment is not special, and an enlightened being is clear that they are not special, not significant, but rather ordinary in the sense that it is evident that we all share the same human experience. What is seeing sees itself in every other human being. This is the source of true compassion. It is useful to cultivate compassion; however, a seer need not cultivate what is already fulfilled.

Evidence of being enlightened is the clear awareness that the persona, ego, identity, who you considered yourself to be prior to "seeing" is inauthentic (not real). You do not have to be viewing from this unconditioned state of being for this to be evident going forward. Once the seed is planted (the seeing has occurred), the fruit of conscious awareness will begin to show up in ways of being and acting, especially in relationship to other human beings.

After seeing, you know the difference between who you turned out to be, given your personal history, and the you that is free to create happiness and well-being. This freedom is transformative in that life occurs as the process of learning to live as an enlightened being: to be as innocent, present, and alive as a baby with the wisdom of a seer.

Will My Bad Habits and Dysfunctional Ways of Behaving End?

Many people consider enlightenment to be the "answer" to all of life's problems. The experience of enlightenment does not change anything. At the same time, the experience of everything changes. When attending to the way of seeing discovered upon enlightenment, everything occurs differently. This is evident when one explores the experience and takes note that, when attending to conscious awareness, perception can be shifted at will to see forms in the field of vision in different ways. For example, when driving a car, riding a bike, or walking, the scenery can be seen as moving past into a void rather than the common view of being in a body that is moving through the scenery. When this is noticed, it is being aware that conscious awareness remains the same, unmoving, experience.

This ability to shift perception is evidence that perception is a virtual phenomenon being generated by the brain based on previous learning. However, once experienced as plastic, this way of seeing can be developed to change the way people, objects, and circumstances occur. Given the existing repetitive patterns of brain activity, the development of this way of seeing requires consistent practice, the implications of such a powerful possibility are difficult to comprehend from the view of a conditioned mind. To put this in simple terms, the potential for change in habitual behavior is evident and far beyond what is possible when one is constrained by the structure of a personality and a limited way of experiencing perception. *So the experience of enlightenment is a doorway to total transformation, but only if the experience is stabilized as a consistent way of experiencing and the necessary determination exercised.*

While the experience of enlightenment is easy, the experience of living from this way of seeing requires a commitment to practice being alert to its presence. Developing the ability to maintain attention this way can be accomplished in a number of ways. Specific meditation techniques are one method of accomplishing this. Another method is to interact and participate in a dialogue with a community where there is an ongoing mutual process of focusing on the exploration and development of seeing, speaking, and acting out of this enlightened state. Any activity that provides the opportunity to exercise this creative experience of perception, such as various art forms, can be utilized to practice seeing, as well. Douglas Harding, mentioned earlier as the creator of a series of "experiments" to give access to "seeing," spoke of the practice as a practice of "staying awake," and mentioned that writing books about the experience was a powerful method for him.

Once the possibility of seeing is realized, it is clear that a new realm of possibility is born. Ways of being and acting that express an unconditioned free natural state begin to appear.

Prior to seeing, you occur for yourself as an identity or personality that turned out a particular way based on upbringing, and the formation of patterns of thinking, feeling, and acting resulting from decisions and conclusions made as a child.

The practice of seeing over time and the expression of this experience with others provides a context for living that actually takes advantage of the neuroplasticity[1] of the brain. Current brain science indicates that simply experiencing a state of flexible, open awareness brings about new neural networks and expands the potential of the brain. This results in an increase in brain activity in the areas of the brain that respond to circumstances with awareness, and less activity in fight or flight networks. Such a shift in brain activity translates into more appropriate, skillful behaviors, and makes a significant difference in human relations.

When attention is directed to the consciously aware experience of seeing, the personality is seen for what it is and is no longer experienced as the self. In fact, the personality and the thought processes and emotional states associated with it occur as subservient to the actual aware consciousness that has been noticed and experienced. This is akin to the servant running the house that is put in his place when the master of the house appears. It brings to mind the last line of the well-known 23rd psalm: And I will dwell in the house of the Lord forever." Further, the notion of self is no longer an accurate way of describing the phenomenon that is seen to be empty and formless, although it is often used as a convention. The idea that we are human beings is simply a reference to our situation. However, upon seeing, it becomes evident that being is that within which the situation is occurring. Human being is appearing in being. Being is the conscious awareness itself and it has no identity; rather, *it is the space in which identity appears*. Pretty cool. When you get this it starts to become evident that something "God like" is happening here.

It is important to stay grounded. If you can get that you have the power of God, and you are just another human being, it is very probable that your dysfunctional ways will change just in the process of life itself.

---

[1] https://en.wikipedia.org/wiki/Neuroplasticity

What Difference Does Being Enlightened Make?

The experience of being enlightened is what one notable fellow referred to as life everlasting. Ultimately, being enlightened is about freedom. It is about the freedom to have everything be as it is. It is the experience that there is nothing to hold onto or let go of. You see, the way it is, is always going to be the way it is and there is never going to be anything we can do about it. I am not talking about the way it could be, or the way we would like it to be, or the way it should be, even the way it will be. I am talking about the way it is. If you notice right now that the way it is, already is, you will notice that this is reality, it is the present, it is all there is, so you might as well say yes to it. The only other possibility is to resist it and suffer. This is not as bad as you might think. Remember that one aspect, *a very important aspect of the way it is, is that it is always changing.* So you see we are never stuck, and it may be that when we, as the Beatles said, "Let it be," it will change naturally toward well-being given that our interference with it, by ignoring it and thinking we know better, is what caused dis-ease. The human brain is an incredible phenomenon. It is capable of generating any virtual reality that can be imagined. While we cannot re-program the brain as a personality because we are limited by what that personality can think and do, we can practice not being a personality by practicing "seeing" and "being." This allows the brain to function in reference to a different way that information coming into the brain is occurring. When we practice actively attending to experience in a relaxed and intensely interested way without resistance to what appears, in time the brain's fear-based neural networks stand down. The incoming data allows the brain to record new and different neural pathways that produce an enlightened experience and promote enlightened behaviors.

After seeing occurs, the play continues and act three begins. In act one, the baby is born and enjoys seeing the wonder of the unnamed world. The baby and the world are one in a dance. In act two the baby forgets being the one and is brought into the world of the many. The world appears in language and the baby becomes a personality and grows up. Growing up involves learning to take life seriously, to make something of yourself, and take on responsibility, to get along and obey the law. Fear is a primary reaction to being in this threatening state where one is confronted by a world of danger.

For most people, life is a two-act play. Act two stretches out over the years and looking forward to retirement becomes a common way of dealing with life for those fortunate enough. Life occurs to be a pattern of wanting, getting, losing, or fearing, resisting, fighting, and avoiding. Many sink into resignation and live with hope through religious beliefs or seeking enlightenment, playing the lottery, or at least surviving cancer. Almost everyone is addicted. Most people are unaware of their addiction to thinking as a way managing life and seek comfort and pleasure at all costs. People do their best but the challenges of life appear overwhelming and happiness is elusive.

If the possibility for a human life is fulfilled, then there is an act three. Act three begins with the experience of enlightenment. The human being discovers seeing again as the baby and has a new experience of life informed by the process of learning to live in the world, yet totally innocent and aware of the timeless nature of consciousness. While nothing changes, everything occurs differently for the seer. The world given by names and concepts occurs as a mere convention for communication, and the direct experience of consciousness shifts into the forefront in a spontaneous movement toward the full realization of experiencing life. This is the realization of the kingdom of heaven on earth.

This consciousness is noticed as the ground of being for living. It occurs as a clearing in which life shows up as a constantly changing mystery. The consciousness that happened in the baby rediscovers itself, and all of the drama and overwhelming confrontations of life are seen as a movie, and as Shakespeare said, "full of sound and fury signifying nothing." And although we continue to lose the recognition that it is a movie, we now know that we can remember, and tend to do so more and more often when things appear grim. This is interesting, in the sense that after the experience of seeing,

the upsets and confrontations of life occur
as opportunities to remember and notice
that, in the moment, as consciousness
(that which is the reality of experience), it is
all just an appearance. This is the context
of being and the power of context.

Why Are So Few People Enlightened?

Given the freedom and possibilities that come with being enlightened, it would seem that everyone who would hear of it would want this experience more than any experience. However, it is apparent that most people are so entranced with the common perception of reality that enlightenment appears to be a rare and unusual experience, or they consider it to be a hoax. In a sense, the possibility that everything that is considered real and important is an illusion is threatening to the house of cards in which most of us live out our lives.

The reason that so few people are enlightened is that it is inconvenient. This may seem strange if enlightenment is an experience that provides freedom and opens the door to seeing the way out of the suffering that seems inherent to life. However, this freedom requires being attentive to every moment with a willingness to experience what Jon Kabat Zinn called the "Full Catastrophe." People strive for stability and certainty and feel threatened by the experience of not having control. Enlightenment is the experience of what Alan Watts called "the wisdom of insecurity." While there is no control or certainty in reality, it is not threatening when it is seen that there is no one to be threatened. The direct experience of consciousness reveals no evidence of the "I" or "me" that is commonly considered the true and only reality. If what is seen upon looking is accepted as a direct experience that is as obvious as the experience of being aware itself, the world as it had previously occurred is no longer valid. This presents an inconvenient truth and begins a process of reorientation. The immediate experience of enlightenment is usually exciting and offers relief from the pressures of life. However, after enlightenment, another world appears that brings the limitations and dysfunction of the personality into focus. This sets off a natural process of working through the changes that come about in ways of being and behaviors.

Most people live in a state of denial. This is not conscious and intentional; it is simply the default state that has continued to be passed on through generations, genetically and through learning and conditioning. This denial is a psychological failure to acknowledge an unacceptable truth or emotion or to admit it into consciousness. It is a defense mechanism that is used to protect the psyche from the stress, confusion, and threat that would occur if not for the turning away. This turning away is ignoring the actual perception of life and being human. It is ignorance, and it is the basis of an unenlightened condition.

For most human beings, the idea that there is something other than what appears to be reality is "spiritual," or religious, and is other than the world in which we live. This is very interesting, in that consciousness does not occur as a physical reality; it is not a "thing" and does not occur "objectively," so it is a mystery to science because it cannot be measured, or even verified to exist. And yet it is the direct experience of being in the world (existing), and is the basis for experience itself. This orientation to the objective physical world is why it is the default state for people to live as a body, a physical entity. We can see a body, and we learn to orient our perception to being in a body, even though it is easy to notice that perception is not always oriented in the body. Take the case of dreaming when we are asleep. We experience being in other places at other times, doing other things, when the body is located in bed. These dreams are experienced as real as they are occurring; however, we relate to this as unreal when we return to what we consider real (come back to being in a body in bed).

Spiritual seekers unwittingly help the rest of world maintain the idea that what there is to experience is an "attainment" that occurs in time. This seeking is a natural and necessary aspect of enlightenment. When the orientation of being a body and a personality becomes uncomfortable enough, the movement to find home begins. In order to become what we are, we must first try to become it in order to realize that it is not necessary to do so.[1] It is like Dorothy in the classic Wizard of Oz: when she clicks her ruby slippers, she awakes at home and can see that she has never left.

So, you could say that actually it is not the case that few people are enlightened. When enlightenment is seen for what it is, it is clear that we are all enlightened; that is, we are all already what we are, and it is simply a matter of looking (clicking those ruby slippers)......and seeing (waking up to what has been there all along).

_____

[1]. Alan Watts, The Supreme Identity, Vintage Books 1972

Once I Am Enlightened, Will I Stay Enlightened?

Once enlightenment is experienced, the door that was never closed is seen as open, and it is evident that there is no such thing as staying enlightened, because you were never not enlightened. Of course, the deeply conditioned habit of being a personality that resides in a body acting out scripts will slip back into place. However, after experiencing enlightenment, it is evident that it is always there, and that if practiced it can be a consistent way of being in life.

In my view the first and perhaps the most essential requirement to take on the practice of living from an enlightened experience is to give up hope. It is the willingness to be brutally honest with yourself about the unworkability of the typical human life. The willingness to acknowledge that when you examine the self-righteous thinking, reactive behaviors, and the buying into a way of living that is clearly failing for humanity, that you are in a condition of detriment. That is, the ability to act in your own best interest is severely limited. It is necessary to notice this and be clear that, as Plato said, "An unexamined life is not worth living."

Without this insight, enlightenment is likely to appear to be some kind of esoteric pyrotechnics akin to psychedelic trips, gurus, and psychic powers. Or the experience may appear interesting but go unrecognized as the possibility of living an extraordinary life and transcending death.

Enlightenment is the discovery of conscious awareness as the ground of being and the recognition that there is no other self. The identification with a name, a body, a personal story is seen to be an *illusion that is maintained by the process of thought.* If enlightenment is claimed by the identity, the enlightened perception shifts into a constrained view again, and enlightenment occurs as a separate special state rather than the natural state of being.

Enlightenment does not occur in time. Time is a linear perception of a reality that only exists in the present. Thought is linear—it occurs one thought at a time, and it creates an illusion of a past and future. It is a convention to serve being in a life and in a world of existence....a life is life-time, and the world occurs as a phenomenon that persists in time. Now is all there is; however, this cannot be perceived and lived without time as its counter aspect. Now could not be perceived without something against which to distinguish it. In fact, all of that which is perceived, all that occurs in the field of human perception, is dependent on its opposite. Up would not occur as up without down. Enlightenment depends on ignorance and identification in order for it to appear distinct and then to be seen as the container of all that exists... this is non-duality....not two. It is form and emptiness as one. Language is inherently a dual phenomenon because it symbolizes experience and thus involves the concept of experience as separate from the experience itself. Concept and experience are then two ways of perceiving. The enlightened perception is no longer separate from the object of perception; they occur as one. This cannot be presented in language; it is exclusively experiential. After the discovery of enlightenment as the ground of being, the ideas presented here are easily understood, because they are simply a matter of noticing the reality of experience.

From an enlightened view, what occurs, if given full attention, occurs as it is, as itself rather than an interpretation, and meaning is seen to be added. It is a state of clarity. Thoughts occur as thoughts rather than perceptions. Feelings occur as physical sensations associated with thoughts. The mind and body are seen as interacting, and conscious awareness is seen as itself rather than confused with a mental process that produces the illusion of a person, with a name, residing in a body. The possibility of true mastery appears. This mastery is a matter of being masterful; that is, being consistently aware of what you are and what is so and living from there, so that it is a natural way of being and a context that uses you in its service. Often, people who have seen the enlightened view refer to their identity as the "little one", or refer to the conventional presentation in the world as the life of the third person rather than the first person, so instead of perceiving the identity as I or me, the identity is perceived as he, or she.

Staying enlightened is a matter of choice. One can choose to practice the way of seeing, being, and acting that is an expression of the reality of conscious awareness. This requires commitment and determination and willingness to experience the deconstruction of the identity, which is a very unpredictable process and typically brings with it a great deal of fear and at times physical discomfort. There are many forms of support and assistance during this process,

especially today in the West where many are offering contemporary forms of teaching that are not encumbered by outdated systems or customs and rituals.

Final Comments

The purpose of this book is to present the possibility of enlightenment as the easiest possible experience a human being can have simply because it is already the case. The words of Douglas Harding are worth repeating here because, in this statement, he is pointing to what this book is about.

"No human, as such, was ever enlightened, for enlightenment is seeing that you aren't so much a human being as just a being. And no being, as such, was ever *un*enlightened, for Being is enlightenment."

-Douglas Harding.

Experiencing enlightenment is not a matter of doing anything to be enlightened but rather a matter of simply noticing that this is the natural, unconditioned, always present state that has gone unnoticed by most of humanity. It is as easy to overlook this perception as it is to notice it, and we are much more accustomed to overlooking it. For example, when doing the pointing experiment, those of us who claim to see nothing and assert that there is nothing to see are actually reporting having seen it. If you report seeing nothing you are reporting seeing your actual nature, even if you will only accept the perception of a thing with form as "reality." If you apply this approach to looking at the sky, you would have to say that the sky does not exist. It has no form; it is not a thing; if you move through it, you encounter nothing. You never hear of pilots reporting that they crashed into the sky. The fact that most human beings continue to ignore the obvious experience and awareness of "be-ing," which precedes "human" being, is itself an interesting situation. It's like everyone is in a movie, and they are so busy playing the roles, so involved in the drama and the story of the movie, doing such a great job of acting, that they totally lost contact with the fact that they are just actors and that it is just a movie. A very few of the actors remember that it is just a movie and try to point it out to the others, but they are too into how the movie is going to turn out, and they all agree that it is the movie that is real, and that there is nothing outside of that. Or, they explain the situation by defining the people who notice that it is just a movie as "special" beings that have attained "enlightenment." The situation is further confused by the fact that so many of the people who claim enlightenment are so willing to be considered special and take advantage of the situation to gain fame or fortune. They sell water by the river, and assist in the perpetuation of the notion that the experience of who we already are and the way it already is, *is not already present*. When you look at it this way, it is hard not to see how foolish this is.

Another way of explaining the oversight that is the usual case for so many human beings is that a large majority of humanity is focused on basic needs, and surviving daily in difficult circumstances, so that it is not easy to give attention to other matters. However, I surmise the most probable explanation for the condition of ignorance that is so pervasive is that most human beings have closed the case on reality. Most human beings live in a condition of "knowing." Most human beings have taken on the "knowledge and beliefs" passed on from prior generations and from parents and schooling as "fact." Most of us operate with the idea that we know who we are and know what is real. Most people are willing to die to defend what they believe to be real and true, or kill others who don't believe. This is the human story. Even with the current science of quantum physics which demonstrates with repeatable experiments that perception is the source of what appears as an objective world, humanity continues to live grounded in a limited science that fits the common view. Just as was the case with the flat world view, since the world did not appear round from the ground view, it was a dramatic shift to accept that it is nonetheless actually the case. In the same sense, the difficulty many of us have when we do the pointing experiment may be due to our looking for something that fits our common beliefs and common knowledge. Something that has a form, something that can be known and understood and fits our expectations. It is like looking at a bowl and not seeing the space in the bowl as the most significant quality of the bowl. Without the space, a bowl would not be a bowl. The space in the bowl allows the bowl to fulfill its existence. The statements about enlightenment throughout this text are intended to draw attention to the experience, and to bring the experience to the forefront of perception. If this experience is perceived, even only for a few moments, there is a new possibility for "seeing" that is available.

The experience of enlightenment is contextual; that is, it has no form but rather determines the perception of form.

The experience of enlightenment is transformative, and is the fulfillment of the human experience. This transformation is the heart of the matter, because it involves a shift from experiencing "self" as a personality or identity, to the experience of awareness in which the self or personality occurs. This awareness is a state of being that is always free, open, and complete, and having access to it gives us the power of transformation. Transformation is the power to cause a shift in experience that frees us from the bondage of time and space and provides the thrill of simply being alive. Such a shift is the fulfillment of the possibility of being human, which is the freedom to be happy in the midst of the full catastrophe.

Enlightenment is a beginning. It is the beginning of truly knowing what you are and what is possible in a human life. Nothing changes after having this experience, and yet everything is different. The possibility of choosing ways of being and acting that are consistent with having a life of fulfillment and love is always present. This possibility is transformation. With enlightenment, it is clear that life is a learning experience and happiness is a choice.

As it turns out, the prison we are in is an illusion; so escaping this prison is unnecessary. All that is required is to give constant attention to the free and open consciousness that is our birthright. Given the habit patterns of the mind and brain, this constant attention requires practice. It has been my experience that the best situation for this practice is the everyday situations and relationships that arise in a human life. Life presents us with challenges that are opportunities to be transformed. Every moment we exist is an opportunity to transform the quality of our life.

If, after doing the experiment and reading through this book, you find that you simply don't get it, or don't see it, and you continue to try and understand or disagree with what is presented here, I suggest that you simply be willing to consider the possibility of enlightenment. Consider returning to this material again to take another shot at it, or take advantage of the multitude of resources available today online to give further consideration to this way of seeing and being. Given what is at stake, your time will be well spent. In particular I recommend visiting the website that continues to offer Douglas Harding's work: (www.headless.org). Here you will find many more experiments that offer many other ways of noticing "seeing," as well as opportunities to interact with others who have utilized the Headless Way to practice seeing and living an enlightened life.

I invite you to be enlightened: to stand for being enlightened and have this stand be the place from which you live.

Some Quotes That Further Elaborate

Werner Erhard on the distinction between the nature of being and our way of being

About the difference between "way of being" *and our* "fundamental and essential nature of being."

"Our way of being is some combination of our mental, emotional, and bodily states, and our thoughts and thought processes and memories. Or saying the same thing in more experiential terms, our way of being is some combination of our attitude or state of mind and our feelings or emotions, plus our body sensations, and our thoughts (and memories) regarding what we are dealing with. That is, our way of being is what is going on with us internally in a given moment or in a given situation ... Being for human beings (the fundamental and essential nature of being for human beings) is "being the clearing (the space, that is, the emptiness) in which the world occurs (shows up)". What shows up in the clearing that we are is all of it, the entire 'state of the world.' All of it (the entire 'state of the world') includes physical objects and non-physical entities of every kind and their properties and in various relationships, others and their properties and in various relationships, and we ourselves and our properties and in various relationships, along with the past, the present, and the future."

Werner continues about the already whole and complete state of human beings:

"The mind is inherently stubborn about change, and seems to snap back to its original position like an elastic band."

Eliezer Sobel author of one of my favorite books *The 99th Monkey* writes about Werner's ideas:

"But there is a catch: when we truly comprehend in our guts the finality and truth that THIS is IT, right now, no matter how our life is, then we grasp what Werner Erhard was always screaming about:

That no magic pill or workshop or

experience of any sort is ever going to come along and finally 'fix' you or me or make us permanently happy, and in that very moment of giving up the search for transformation, a transformation paradoxically does in fact occur.

One recognizes that one was never broken in the first place, and suddenly all the energy previously devoted to seeking a way out of or through the problem of the unfulfilled self is freed up to power one's mission and vision, which is a gesture of giving and contribution rather than one of searching, waiting, and hoping.

And that is a good thing, if a bit sobering, because it means we are asked to step up to the plate in life with what and who we already are. We have been given our piece in the game, and it only remains to play wholeheartedly."

NOTE:

Ramana Maharishi is currently considered to be a unique example of enlightenment because his experience occurred without any connection to any system or teaching. His father died when he was a teenager,

*and because he was terrified of death, he
laid down and pretended to be dying.
During this experience, he came to see the
actual nature of his conscious awareness.*

Taken from a description of his writing:

"Therefore what Sri Ramana means in this
first paragraph by the term 'knowledge-
investigation "who am I?"' is not a mere
intellectual analysis of our knowledge 'I
am,' but is an actual examination or deep
scrutiny of our fundamental knowledge or
consciousness 'I am' in order to know
through direct experience what it really is.
Such an investigation or scrutiny cannot be
done by thinking, but only by turning our
attention back on ourself to know our own
essential consciousness of being. When
our attention or power of knowing is turned
outwards to know things other than ourself,
it becomes our thinking mind, but when it
turns back inwards to know our essential
self, it remains in its natural state as our
essential self – that is, as our true non-dual
self-conscious being."

-Sri Ramana Maharshi

The Interview was conducted with KQED,

San Francisco, hosted by Michael Toms
MT is Michael Toms and WE is Werner
Erhard.

NOTE:

*While this segment of an interview with
Werner Erhard may seem difficult to follow,
it is the only time I have come across
Werner directly pointing to the what
Douglas Harding's work and the essence of
Zen points to. Werner presents this
pointing in a unique way that addresses the
typical Western mindset, and fact that most
people don't ask about "IT" (The direct
reality of being, or "Who we are") In the est
training back in the seventies "getting it"
was considered the result of the training.
This interview took place during that
period. The est training was considered by
many to be a two week approach to
enlightenment.*

MT: I'd like to talk a little bit about the "IT,"
getting "IT;" now, you got "IT," and a lot of
us would like "IT," now what the hell is "IT?"
In other words, what's it all about as far as
you're concerned?

WE: First off, I want to tell you that the answer to what "IT" is, cannot be contained in the system from which the question comes. As a child, I asked how far out did the sky go? I thought maybe it stopped at the clouds at first and somebody said no, and I thought maybe it stopped, you know, some place out there, and they said, no, it's endless. So I said, "Endless, let's see now, how far out is endless, well, at the end of endless there must be a wall and it stops there, oh I got it." But then I said, "Well, wait a minute, how far out does the wall go?", and then "Well, no, the wall has to stop someplace, so there must be another space . . ." and you get into that mind-boggling. And I use the word mind-boggling as a technical term because the notion of infinity is mind-boggling. The only way the mind can deal with the notion of infinity is, to turn it into a symbol, it can't deal with it as an event. Now, what "IT" is, is an event which the mind cannot deal with, so I cannot give you a mindful answer. That doesn't mean I can't answer it; the problem is that the answer I give you will be mind-boggling, plus the fact that nobody's asking the question. You see, you've just asked a question which nobody cares about. You go around telling people what "IT" is and they say, "Well, you're crazy," you know, it's meaningless until somebody's asked the question.

But let me answer what "IT" is, now that I've told you I can't answer it. What "IT" is is you; in other words, you are what "IT" is. That doesn't mean what it sounds like it means, for a couple of reasons: First off, you aren't who you think you are. So if I say, you are what "IT" is, and you think that you are something that you aren't, then that's misleading. Secondly, if you attempt to put that information (that you are what "IT" is) into a system I call the mind, the system won't contain it; it can't deal with curved lines, it can only deal with straight lines, so to speak. Now is when "IT" is, here is where "IT" is, and you are what "IT" is, and the you which is what "IT" is, is not some role you've chosen to play nor is it some position, you are not "over there." That's just your representation which is over there; you're perhaps all over the place or no place or.....but you see that's mind boggling to say that you are everywhere and nowhere. What does that mean? That's crazy. At least, it's crazy in a system which won't contain the information. It would be totally rational in a system which could contain the information. All rational means is it fits with the set of agreements that we are using to look at the thing. So, to get even more specific about what "IT" is—"IT" is you experiencing yourself without any symbology or any concept. Normally, I experience myself through my thoughts; I think who I am. Sometimes I experience myself through my body; I sense who I am. Sometimes I experience myself through my emotions; I feel who I am. **Well, "IT" is you experiencing you directly without any intervening system. (My Bold)**

NOTE:

J.Khrisnamirti championed the idea that one must pursue and discover the truth of awareness for oneself. He abandoned the opportunity to be hailed as a world teacher and stated "The Truth is a Pathless Land." In his talks he challenged people to question the conditioned state of mind that pervades humanity.

Quote from J. Khrisnamirti

"Our consciousness has been programmed for thousands and thousands of years and we have been conditioned, programmed, wired...to be, to think as individuals. To think as separate entities struggling, struggling conflict -- from the moment you're born until you die. We are programmed to it. We have accepted that. We have never challenged it, we have never asked if it possible to live a life totally, absolutely without conflict.

"And the religious organizations throughout the world have maintained this individual salvation. And we are questioning very seriously whether there is an individual consciousness. Whether you as a human consciousness have a separate consciousness from the rest of mankind. You have to answer this. You can not just play with it. My consciousness and yours; if we've been brought up, programmed conditioned to the individual then my consciousness is all this activities of thought. Fear is thought..."

The suffering, the anxiety, the uncertainty, the deep regrets, wounds, the burden of centuries of sorrow is part of thought. Thought is responsible for all this."

- J. Khrisnamurti

NOTE:

This piece is a description of the path that
lies beyond the initial experience of seeing.
I have not focused on this in this book
other than mentioning the process of living
from enlightenment that becomes possible
after seeing. I thought it might be of interest
to those who have an interest in this path.

The path of the Mystic
is beyond words.

It is a fall into
the Heart of Darkness
in which the self
is sacrificed
over and over again.

The mystic dies into God
and yet returns to the World
to offer the self
as the ultimate sacrifice.

This offering serves the totality,
it is the giving of formlessness to form
so that form may come
to know its own true nature.

It is the Tantra of Life.

It is the way of the Mystic.

When chaos appears in your World,
when disturbance appears in your mind,
when desolation appears in your emotional
body,

do not turn away
assuming that there
has been some mistake,

do not try to bury that
which hurts in the recesses
of your consciousness.

For this that appears
so dark and dangerous
is in fact an offering of light,

it is a call for Death
that allows a resurrection.

In the surrender
to complete annihilation
of that part of you
that clings to an idea of self-identity
based on a picture created in the mind,

there is a relaxation
around the terror of non-existence.

This relaxation allows
all false concepts of self
 even ones that provide

a sense of security as the "I"
to be offered into
the fire of transmutation.

Out of the ashes of this offering,
arises the phoenix
with wings of gold.

This is the birth
of a new
awakened consciousness,
more transparent
and more luminous
than anything you could
imagine yourself to be.

When all hell breaks loose,
my friend, do not waste
this opportunity for falling into
the arms of the Beloved.

For this is
who you truly are.

- Amoda Maa Jeevan

NOTE:

*Alan Watts was one of the first to introduce
Zen to the West. His book* The Supreme

Identity *has been my favorite presentation on the nature of enlightenment for decades.*

To ask "How can I attain realization?" is the wrong question, if by "I" is meant the ego, for the Self, not the ego realizes . If by "I" is meant the Self, the question is absurd, because the Self does not need to realize on account of its inherent and essential infinity. Realization comes only when the Self wills it freely, without necessity. Can we then do nothing?

The Self will not let us do nothing. As soon as we begin to desire realization, this the sign that the process has begun. Our search for the Self is moved by the Self. To become, or realize, what we are, we must first try to become it , in order to realize effectively that it is not necessary to do so.

God, as the Self, is known interiorly, as the inmost subject, for the subjective realm is not opposed to the objective, whereas objects are mutually exclusive. Hence the perfect compatibility of realization with everyday experience.

-Alan Watts

Another great quote from Douglas Harding where he specifically points to enlightenment.

"Seeing what you really are is just about the easiest thing in the world to do, and just about the most difficult to keep doing – at first. Normally, it takes months and years and decades of coming back home, to the spot one occupies (or rather, doesn't occupy – the world does that) before one learns the knack of remaining centered, of staying indoors, of living from one's space instead of from one's face. Nevertheless, now you know how to get there, you can visit home whenever you wish and whatever your mood. And, once over the threshold, you're perfectly at home: here, you can't put a foot wrong. Practice doesn't make perfect here: it is perfect from the start. You can't half see your facelessness now, or see half of it. **There are no degrees of enlightenment: it is all, or nothing.**" (My bold)

-Douglas Harding

I specifically formatted this in a larger font to emphasize the significance of context as the key to transformation. I think this is a great quote to end with. I highly recommend looking Paul Hedderman up on YoutTube.

Awareness is the context of life. What you incorrectly call "self" is the content.

-Paul Hedderman

Further Thoughts (following publication)

Following publication of this book, I had the opportunity to re-read my work many times for editing. I also had the opportunity to hear many responses and reactions to the book. Most of the feedback was good, and it was evident that many found the book very useful in terms of opening up the idea of enlightenment.

As I stated in the introduction, the inspiration for the book came from conversations with people around the world in video conference meetings with Richard Lang, who along with his brother David, are the guardians and carriers of the teachings of Douglas Harding.

It wasn't that enlightenment or the experience of "seeing," or "being" was new to me when I came into contact with

Richard and this online community, but these conversations provided a place to explore the experience and share the world of possibilities that come along with being enlightened.

To be in conversations across time and space with people who are speaking from a common experience of this way of "seeing" and "being," called "The Headless Way," was and continues to be one great and fun way of practicing what it is to be truly "human." This way of being that attends to the way we really are and the way our seeing actually occurs is what being enlightened is all about. One thing that is unique about this community is that it is not "special" or esoteric. People are just talking about the immediate experience of seeing and sharing points of view and interpretations of this mysterious situation in which we all find ourselves.

As the conversations continue and I continue to practice not being what I am not, I am finding that this life is more of an incredible trip than I ever imagined. I have come to see that, without anything changing, everything is different. What was an annoyance is now just what is happening. What was a confusing, disturbing, and troublesome past no longer exists. What was a threatening future is now an opportunity to create. It is such a powerful realization to be clear that life only exists "now." Life is "now," and all of life is just "now." "Being" is noticing this moment. *It is all just "now."*

This is not to say that enlightenment is just bliss. That is one of the misconceptions that has led to much confusion.

Once *what we **actually are** is seen*, reality can be known; in fact, I have heard a number of teachers define spirituality as making contact with and being familiar with "reality." Simply said, reality is what is happening, which is always in the moment of now, and is empty of any actual "person." Yet it continues to involve appearing as a person in the world, with a body, in relationship to all other people.

SO….after enlightenment is recognized, the brain continues to play the habit patterns encoded in the neurons, and *the game is on.*

Now that we know that the brain is plastic—that is, the brain is constantly changing and encoding new neuro-patterns or reinforcing old patterns according to perceptions and felt experiences—we can begin to practice using mindfulness exercises to change the brain.

This is a revolutionary and profound opening for creating a new realm of expression in behavior and a fulfillment of the quality of being awake in the world which is best described as "joy."

We now have scientific evidence[1] that

basic secular mindfulness practice, if done consistently over time (as little as eight weeks), changes the brain in significant ways. Dr. Richard Davidson, who has led the research in this area, suggests that we give serious consideration to the research that indicates that we are mostly "unwittingly" shaping our brain's networks by what we attend to, and by how we are attending. This means we are mostly "practicing" mindlessness, and replaying the individual and collective fear-based, reactive "habit" patterns.

The consistent formal practice of mindfulness via sitting or moving meditation over time will produce a consistent state of mindfulness that is the realization of enlightenment in who we are being and how we are acting in the world.

Therefore, the path to living an enlightened life is practice.

PRACTICE.

noun
1 the actual application or use of an idea, belief, or method as opposed to theories about such application or use.

verb *[with obj.]* (*Brit.* **practise**)
1 perform (an activity) or exercise (a skill) repeatedly or regularly in order to improve or maintain one's proficiency

We have been practicing human being, rather that being human. We inherited an identity: the identity of humanity. Our brains have neuro patterns that are replications of generations of the same fears, same longings, same view of life and reality. Those who experienced liberation from this condition were considered religious icons, esoteric masters, or mystics. We now live in a world in which the veil of illusion can easily be dissolved by anyone who chooses to do so. Teachers and practices from around the world from the beginning of video and audio recording are now readily available on the internet. Most of humanity has or will have access to many of the greatest teachers and masters. We have access to the greatest university of wisdom ever available to humanity.

PRACTICE WHAT?

Mindfulness is a word commonly used to describe it. I have found that it amounts to "practice attention, and practice love." What I mean by love is the way you see what you are attending to. To give attention to what occurs in the field of perception with love is to give attention without conditions; to give attention to whatever appears in the world and in the mind with complete acceptance, appreciation, and gratitude. It is to do this out of trusting that which is beyond our little mind and to give attention to that which is infinite and beyond comprehension, beautiful in all it's glory; *the realm of all possibility*.

This can be thought of as a spiritual practice, but we live in a time when we are coming out of the need to be interested in "mysticism." What is *"actual" need not be related to as esoteric or mystical.* This has taken us down a rabbit hole for long enough.

No curtain, no veil, no wizard of Oz. Just "This."

Of course GOD has not intended to fool us, or herself. In order for love to exist, GOD had to let there be lovers (embodied, individual beings).

Are you willing to be a lover? A lover of life and truth? If "yes," then are you willing to be Love?

If you say "YES." Then you have to deal with the brain. Because the brain has been programmed for "NO." And the mind from which the brain got programmed, the mind of all of humanity, is still coming out of a primal, survival, fear based state.

So to train the brain is to practice. This practice has two parts.

One: Be what you are; that is, pay attention as *awareness itself attending.*

Two: Act consistent with what you are. Express through speech and actions that which is appropriate to the situation and consistent with Love.

The entrainment and total virtual container that we have been "being" is so complete for most of us that what I have been saying for many will occur as nonsense. However, even for those of us who "get it," being fully committed and doing the practice is "improbable." I have studied this and experimented with my own mind and it is clear to me that *this practice has to be the basis of one's life* to interrupt the patterns that play out in thoughts, feelings, and behaviors.

This is evident if one listens to the great teacher J. Khrisnamurti speak to audiences, especially in his last years. He was clearly frustrated and impatient with the state of mind common to most people. He is said to have shared just prior to his death that he did not think anyone heard him.

This is a very difficult aspect of the conversation for what is possible in a human life. To be a passionate force of love in a realm of confusion, mistrust, hatred, and despair, is a heroic stand; *not a stand that an ego would take*.

It takes a willingness to see the existence that passes for a human life as a *crucible*.

Most of us think life itself is the thing....that getting the most out of life is what matters, you know, what we have, what we want, how it goes, how it turns out, blah, blah, blah.

Life is just a vehicle for "being." It is what is happening, and it is empty of any inherent meaning or purpose. It happens in time and space and includes death.

Being isn't conceivable and is not in time or space. Being is the space of all possibility. It is the already, and is eternal enlightenment. Given that it is already as it is; complete, fulfilled, and includes all possibility, ……it is easy.

TAKE IT EASY.

Love.
David

---

[1] http://centerhealthyminds.org/science/overview

About the Author

Since early on in my life, I had a strong sense that I was more than my circumstances. This led me through many turns in the road of life, some of which were useful and some of which were very painful and difficult. On several occasions during my early adult years, I stumbled into a distinctly different state of consciousness that was so complete and fulfilling in every way that I was certain that this was a possible experience that could be accessed. It was as if the experience was one in which I was totally myself, with full knowledge of life, with a calm loving and joyful interest in all that appeared before me. For most of my life, I have considered this experience to be what is called enlightenment. Only recently, as a natural experience took hold, have I come to see that this is simply one of the states of mind available in a life, and that it is often confused with the natural experience one has after recognizing an authentic ground of being. As my life continued after completing undergraduate school, I took a job at a maximum security prison as a basic education teacher and counselor. The world inside the prison was so brutal and bizarre that it shook me deeply, and I felt a commitment to somehow help the prisoners to realize an experience of freedom from suffering. I ended up working 32 years in prisons as a counselor, a psychologist, and for the last 12 years as an assistant warden and then warden. I implemented and personally led programming for prisoners during this time to provide access to the teachings of the East and the new teachings appearing in the West that offered freedom. Over these years I studied and practiced meditation, and read the works of many of the Eastern and Western teachers. Some of the works that influenced me the most were the writings of Carlos Castaneda, Alan Watts, J. Krishnamurti, and George Gurdjieff. Since 1973, I have been a student of Werner Erhard's work because of his unique ability to create new paradigms of language and thought that have proven to be very powerful in building upon the existing work in the area of human consciousness. Today, with access to a multitude of teachers via the internet, I have spent a large portion of my time studying the most current expressions and conversations about the possibilities for the fulfillment of a human life. Since leaving the prison career I have continued with a small psychology practice, started providing consultation and training to psychologists, and created writing projects to make this new work available on a larger scale. The heart of my work today is the utilization of forty years of a combination of conventional psychological approaches with new leading edge work in human transformation and Leadership. I feel privileged to be a voice for a new future. It has become clear to me that the true gift in life is the experience of making a difference in the lives of others and contributing to the well-being of all of humanity.

NOTES